TENNIS

coordination, rhythm and timing of champions

THE DEVIN-ADAIR COMPANY

NEW YORK   1962

CONTENTS

1 *Why this book was written* 1

2 *Motion economy in tennis—nine rules* 8

3 *The ballistic swing* 11

4 *Grips* 18

5 *The backhand* 21

6 *The forehand* 34

7 *The serve* 45

8 *The volley* 55

9 *The Auxiliary strokes* 60

10 *How to watch the ball* 66

11 *Strategy* 68

12 *Equipment* 77

13 *The ball trap* 83

14 *Pros and cons* 86

15 *Summary:* 50 *things to remember* 102

Conclusion: What this system does for you 106

INSTANT TENNIS

1.

Why this book was written

It seems odd that up until now no one has called attention to the fact that "name" tennis players teach one method and play according to another. Book after book, thirty or forty of them, authored by these stars of the tennis court, and photo after photo of them—both action pictures and posed ones—plus observations at Newport, Longwood, and Forest Hills clearly prove this to be the case.

Why is this so? The players themselves, when asked this question, often reply, "The way I play is for experts and should be used only by experienced players. It should not be attempted by beginners—they should wait until they have played many years."

But I do not agree, and for two reasons. First, on theoretical grounds, I believe that a beginner learning anything should learn it correctly from the start, to avoid the formation of bad habits. And secondly, on practical grounds, it has been my experience in teaching tennis that the correct stroking, which the experts would reserve for themselves, can be taught to beginners with completely and rather startingly satisfactory results. I have taught pupils who had never played tennis before in their lives, and within five minutes had them hitting backhands with the actual footwork and the swing of the champions. This is not to say that all their shots were perfect, for precision in tennis comes from long practice against all the variables in the bounce of the ball. But their shots, if not perfect, were fundamentally *correct*—for they were using the stroke of the champion; they were using what I call the Ballistic Swing.

Now, it would be both untrue and ungenerous to state that our big name players are deliberately advocating a method of teaching tennis that has no practical use in 98% of the shots they themselves make in actual play. I am convinced, from reading the books they have written and from personal conversations with some of these players themselves, that they are leading this "double life" for five reasons:

1. They play well instinctively and have never really analyzed their own games.

2. Because of this analytical lack, they have good-naturedly and unresistingly accepted some of the fallacies about the game that have sprung up over the past half-century and have by now grown so set that they have quite obliterated certain fundamental truths from their minds.

3. There is a great love of tradition among tennis players as well as resistance to scientific attitudes. I love tradition, too, but not to the point where I can stand by and see hundreds, even thousands, of eager potential tennis players, discouraged by frustration and poor teaching, turn to some other sport. I would like to see tennis tradition based on a logical approach to the game.

4. And there is the mistaken idea that great players are naturally great teachers. Such is rarely the case, and this blind devotion to our heroes of the court causes us to accept their opinions on every matter. Carried to absurdity, we allow a heavyweight boxing champion to tell us how to vote in presidential elections.

5. Photographs taken of the great players have been consistently misleading. There are three types of photographs: those specially posed for

tennis books or magazines, where the player is most anxious to assume the "classic stance" for exhibit; those of which the photographer is particularly proud, not because the stroke was good but because it was a feat of photographic skill to capture it on film—the impossible "get" or the dynamic action shot, where the player looks as though he has slipped on a cake of soap emerging from the shower. And third, those pictures of the basic run-of-the-mill tennis shots that occur 98% of the time on the court, but are pretty well kept out of the news media because they violate the mistaken but sacred idea of how the game should be played.

It is my belief that a teacher of tennis should have the same scientific, systematized training that every qualified teacher in our school systems should have, and that the wrong approach to teaching tennis, besides wasting time and money, can actually be harmful to the pupil, who often would be better off if allowed to obey his own instincts. Much of the racket-throwing by our Davis Cup players may be attributed to frustrations brought on by our failure to teach correct fundamentals. When our top players show how to hit a forehand for a tennis magazine and then never use the same stance once during a match, it could help produce these temper tantrums.

One of the first benefits derived from our scientific approach to learning tennis is that the pupil is not taught bad habits for several years and then asked to unlearn them. It is manifestly better to inculcate good habits from the very beginning. These good habits are firmly grounded in the principles of motion economy, starting with the classification of hand, wrist, arm, and body movements. Knowledge of these four "class" motions enables the teacher, and ultimately the pupil, to analyze his game and check each component part of his stroke for possible faults.

An example of the application of these motion principles is the pupil's awareness that he is using a fourth-class (body) motion on the drive when he should be taking the ball waist-high with a third-class motion that is easier, more effective, and less tiring. Balls at the net could be blocked with a first-class hand motion and to impart spin, wrist and hand could be used for more speed. Most net shots, however, require a third-class motion involving the forearm.

Our scientific method of teaching makes the player's stroking automatic, freeing him of worry about mechanics and permitting him to devote all his attention to strategy. Because this method is based on natural sequence, it is more easily remembered. Logical habit simplifies all movements, makes them automatic and diminishes fatigue.

Tennis is a beautiful game, with enough intrinsic value to justify its merits. But it is also used by athletes in other sports for conditioning because it is fast, rhythmic, and uniquely challenging.

Whether we like it or not, we are living in an age of great tensions, and now, more than ever, we need the mental relaxation and physical stimulation that we can get from tennis well-played. This book is not intended to create a class of players contemptuously known as "tennis bums," but to make the learning of a wonderful game available to all who might enjoy it and to develop natural talents to their greatest proficiency in the shortest possible time.

In this approach to the teaching of what the greatest instinctive players of the world have been doing since tennis began, I have applied my considerable training in motion study. It was the application of this same knowledge that enabled me to win the New England Senior Championship in 1957 and 1958, and to acquire a national ranking, even though my success on the court prior to that time had been only mediocre and would have relegated me to complete anonymity if I had continued to use the methods prescribed in other books.

Chapters 15 and 16 and the check-charts are designed to guide a parent, friend, or another inexperienced tennis player in helping a pupil spot and correct weaknesses in the basic elements of stroking. Refinements, of course, will come naturally through practice. We first ask the reader to learn the principle behind each stroke.

This method of teaching will considerably reduce the time now needed to learn the game. The day is gone when tennis pros feel they need to say, "This girl has been improving over the last eight years—next year we will teach her to turn her shoulder." Today's students can learn to turn their shoulders in the very first lesson. They will play better, they will play longer, and they will play with more enjoyment.

Here's to the world's greatest game!

2.
Motion economy in tennis—nine rules

In this book, I have attempted to analyze and explain the basics of good tennis according to the principles of motion economy as applied to the human body when it is engaged in athletics. A great deal has already been done in the field of motion study so far as industrial use is concerned, but its application to the proper and most efficient use of the various parts of the human body in the playing of our most popular sports has been curiously and sadly neglected. This book is a venture in the correction of that situation.

An explanation of all the principles of motion

economy, even in a general way, would consume another volume; and since it is my present purpose to confine them to their usefulness in the learning of tennis, I have omitted any mention of them that is not absolutely necessary to an intelligent understanding of the game. Moreover, while the principles involved have not usually been specifically mentioned in their relation to the various kinds of tennis strokes, they form the scientific basis of my teaching as set forth in the following pages.

Anyone wishing to do further research in the field of motion economy (and it is a rewarding study) should read *Time and Motion Study,* by Ralph M. Barnes, M.E., Ph.D., or any of the excellent books by Frank Gilbreth dealing with the same broad subject.

So far as the present book is concerned, I feel that a brief mention of the following nine rules, as they pertain to the playing of tennis, will suffice:

1. Motions should be confined to the lowest classification with which it is possible to hit the ball satisfactorily (e.g. eliminating the use of the whole arm if a motion of the wrist will serve as well or better).
2. Ballistic movements, which go on their own momentum from an initial spring, are faster, easier, and more accurate than restricted or controlled move-

ments (which require conscious muscular control throughout), and should be employed at all times if possible.

3. Continuous, curved motions should be used in preference to straight-line motions involving sudden and sharp changes in direction, which call for a change in muscular reflexes and waste time as well as energy.

4. Rhythm is essential to the smooth and automatic performance of any stroke, and the ball should be hit at the right place to permit easy and natural rhythm wherever possible.

5. Momentum of swing should be employed to assist the player whenever possible, thus reducing muscular effort; but in cases where momentum is an obstacle to be overcome by muscular effort, it should obviously be kept at a minimum.

6. The ball's momentum should be used wherever possible to obtain power with a minimum of effort.

7. Both the arms should not be idle at the same time, except during rest intervals.

8. Both arms should begin as well as complete their movements at the same instant.

9. Your arm motions should be in opposite and symmetrical directions, and should be made simultaneously (relative to serve only).

3.

The ballistic swing

One of the first things a tennis teacher will tell his pupils is "Stand sideways to the net and keep your eye on the ball." By sideways, they further explain, they mean that the feet should be pointing to the sidelines and parallel to the baseline. "Always get in this position as soon as you know the direction of the ball," they coach persistently. Not only is this illustrated pictorially in all the tennis books, but the text will ask the beginner to pivot on the ball of his right foot (for the forehand) and step over with the left so that it is parallel to the right foot. This system has been taught to children in every clinic I have watched, and it is known as the "classic stance" in tennis jargon.

What has further confused these writers of tennis manuals is the fact that they believe the sideways position is necessary because Ted Williams stands sideways to the plate in baseball. But they completely overlook the fact that Ted Williams has to hit down either foul line, and the action of his wrists is a different one from that used in tennis.

Similarly, it has been pointed out, fallaciously, that Ben Hogan stands sideways to the golf ball, and therefore the sideways stance is desirable in tennis, too. But Hogan stands sideways because he can swing back with the pivot and keep both eyes on the ball to make a drive. On the approach shots, he will point his feet towards the flag on the green, and it is here, rather than in the drive, that the footwork approximates that of the correct tennis player.

However, the golf swing as taught today is open to question. Not long ago, I visited Dave Rosen, who owns the Golf Trading Company in New York, and showed him the film "Tennis for Everybody," which was put out by the United States Lawn Tennis Association. It was their latest teaching film, in which tennis notables took turns in showing the "right" method. It was cosponsored by the Eastern Tennis Patrons and the Chicago Parks District, and depicted at length the "recommended" techniques as demonstrated by Mercer Beasley, Eddie Moylan (the West Side Tennis Club pro), Judy Barta (USLTA Clinic Chairman), Maureen Connolly, Cap Leighton and John Conroy (Princeton coach).

But that picture also shows Darlene Hard playing Maria Bueno in the National Championships at Forest Hills. And here the announcer asks the viewer to note the similarity between these champions' playing technique and that shown in the previous, teaching half of the film. The irony of it is that when this film is shown on a "film editor," which allows the viewer to stop the action at any given point, it is only too obvious that Bueno and Hard are doing just the opposite of what is "taught" in the previous section of the same film!

When I showed this film to Dave Rosen, he started to look for parallels in golf. Standing with his feet *pointed toward the canvas backstop* in one of his golf cages, he began to hit ball after ball straight into the center of the canvas, using one hand. He was frankly amazed at the accuracy of his swing, even though the golf club he was using was not originally designed and weighted for one-handed play. I had tried a similar stance at the driving range the previous summer, using two hands, and also got amazing accuracy. My swing was completely free of the hook and slice that come from hitting "inside-out" as the golf pro teaches. My stroke kept the club-head directly behind the ball, and my longer follow-through was straight along the line of flight. I used a shorter backswing and a longer follow-through from that position.

During Little League practice with my two boys, then aged nine and eleven, I found they were having difficulty getting the bat around fast enough. By pointing the toe of the right foot between first and second base, instead of to the right of first base, they were able to swing the bat around faster. This pointing of the toes resulted in a shortened backswing, and gave more spring action. In no time at all, they began to hit the ball out of the infield with a power that was not apparent before. We then taught this to other young baseball players with amazing results.

Karl Rittman, the illustrator of this book, is the perennial Rhode Island Badminton Doubles Champion, in addition to being one of our top sports artists. He tells me that all his overheads are hit *with the toes pointing towards the net,* and that by advancing the right foot prior to hitting the smash, he can generate much more power.

In the March, 1961, issue of *Scholastic Coach,*

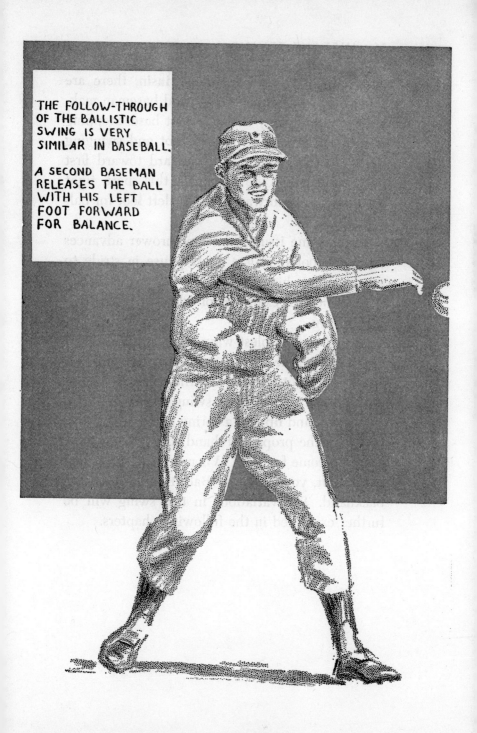

THE FOLLOW-THROUGH OF THE BALLISTIC SWING IS VERY SIMILAR IN BASEBALL.

A SECOND BASEMAN RELEASES THE BALL WITH HIS LEFT FOOT FORWARD FOR BALANCE.

edited by idea man Herman Masin, there are some excellent photos of a second baseman making the double-play throw to first base. Stepping on second base with the left foot and swinging the right foot around and forward toward first base, he releases the ball from this short, tight pivot and steps forward with his left foot for balance.

In the same issue, a javelin thrower advances his right foot during a short pause in stride to get power into his throw.

These are all examples of what I call the Ballistic Swing.

One of the simplest ways to learn this motion in its most basic form is to stand with the feet apart and pivot the body to the left and then to the right, letting the arms swing naturally. When you are wound up like a spring on the right side, you have the proper forehand form to allow the swing to come forward. When you are wound up to the left, you have the Ballistic Swing on the backhand. The variations in this swing will be further explained in the following chapters.

THE FOLLOW-
THROUGH OF THE
BALLISTIC SWING

4.

Grips

So much has been written about grips that a mere mention of their purpose it all that is needed here.

In the standard or so-called Eastern forehand grip, most of the surface of the palm is behind the racket. In the backhand grip, the back of the hand is on top of the racket handle. For the backhand drive, place the thumb along the back of the handle.

Some players claim that a grip in between these positions is the best one, because it obviates the need to change grips for each kind of shot. While this "Continental" grip does simplify things, the result is a compromise for each type of shot

GRIPS:
(left)
EASTERN FOREHAND
USED BY MAJORITY
OF PLAYERS.

(right)
USUAL BACKHAND

and is not best from the point of view of power. Changing grips is really no problem if the player uses the left hand to hold the racket while rotating the right hand on the racket handle.

If left to nature, the right hand's normal position is with the palm down, when brought to the backhand side, and the palm in back of the racket when it is on the right side. Using the V formed by the thumb and first finger as a guide on the racket is not an accurate method, as the length of the fingers will affect this V, throwing the player off from his truly correct grip. Place the racket at right angles to the flight of the ball, and then observe the grip that feels most comfortable in that position.

Grips are largely dependent on the height of the ball, which in turn is determined mostly by the surface that you use. The so-called Western grip was developed on the concrete courts of California. It is no longer much used.

5.
The backhand

The backhand should be the easiest stroke to learn, because the body is out of the way. Those who are afraid of the backhand should remember that cards are dealt with a similar motion (not a very difficult feat) and that all of the hard shots in Judo are hit backhanded. When carefully analyzed, the backhand emerges as a graceful and easy swing, completely in accord with the natural motions of the human body. The idea that the backhand is a difficult and unnatural stroke, requiring years of practice at complex and contradictory techniques, is a myth that has sprung out of faulty analysis of the stroke and has been nurtured over the years by over-complication in teaching. It is important to master this stroke early, for those who do not will find themselves running around backhand shots and using forehands in their place.

The pivot is the most important element in the backswing. Toes point to the net—or net post—and hips and shoulders coil and uncoil completely.

There are two directions the racket may take in the backhand: either it may start from a point below the flight of the ball and travel to a position above it, as in the top-spin backhand drive; or it may be hit from an above-the-flight-of-the-ball position—the backhand chop or slice. Balls hit at the top of the rise are generally sliced, because it is safer. When the ball can be taken low, the top-spin backhand is used.

The backhand grip is a one-quarter turn from the Eastern forehand—or to put it another way, the back of the hand faces up on the top plane of the handle while the racket face is perpendicular to the ground. The pupil will soon learn the correct position by playing. It is impossible to find it by the usual V method, since, as stated before, this does not take into consideration the length of the fingers or the size of the palm.

Again, the important point is the position of the feet. Most other books about tennis advocate that the player stand sideways to the net, with the feet pointing toward the sidelines. This does not allow for a ballistic swing—unless the back is turned to the net when one does not have enough time, even if that position were a means to extra power. But it isn't; by the time the racket contacts the ball, the swing forward is practically over, which means that all the power has been dissipated on the backswing and the swing *prior* to hitting the ball.

So, with the racket held in the backhand grip and the feet in ready position, turn the shoulders, arm, and racket back to where the trunk swing is tightened. The left hand remains on the racket close to the right during the backswing, aiding the stroke and making for a sounder swing. This is what some golfers call the one-piece swing. If the swing back, with the feet parallel and pointing to the net, seems uncomfortable, it is permissible to advance the right foot slightly, or point the toes more parallel to the baseline.

When the racket is back at waist height, horizontal to the ground, step forward toward the net with the right foot and start the shoulders, racket and arm turning forward simultaneously; contact the ball opposite or slightly ahead of the right foot. Follow through forward until you can swing no further. Be sure the swing is a continuous swing from beginning to end, without any jerk. Don't swing forward halfway and then stop the racket just before the ball is hit, as some beginners have a tendency to do. The swing is smooth, the ball is also hit smoothly, and immediately after contact the racket may be speeded up, but this should be done smoothly also, without any jerkiness to disturb the direction or the spin of the ball.

When a ball comes in far out to the left, sidestep or sideskip over to the ball, and you are in the basic position. While sidestepping, be sure you are getting your racket back so that when you do arrive, you are ready to swing forward without hurrying the backswing. Should you have to get to the ball more quickly, you may cross over with the right foot, but this is for emergency only and should not be considered a standard maneuver. It is also permissible to run straight for the sidelines, but if you do, be sure you land on the left foot with the toe as much toward the net as possible. This toe position restricts the backswing and a shorter backswing makes for greater accuracy.

In all returns of service, or when the ball is too deep, a step is not only unnecessary, but actually weakens the return. When playing against a weak serve, stand in on the return and take the ball on the rise or at the top of the bounce. But never step forward with the right foot, until after the ball has been hit and you wish to follow your return to the net. A slight advance of the left foot adds power to your return. With practice, you should be able to hit your backhand return cross-court or down the line with the feet pointing to the net. This is not only a true ballistic return, but it is a stance which will reveal nothing to your opponent about which direction your return will take. Should the server follow his serve to the net, place your return just over the net, mostly to his backhand side. This will make him hit up and you are then in a good position to smash, lob over his head or pass him on either side.

Should the serve be out of reach, it is permissible to cross over with your right foot and block the ball. However, this is the position that should be avoided if possible, as you are not only in a bad position if you have to run to the other side of the court for his next return, but the cross-over position makes you swing with a quick arm motion, and the power from the body is lacking, thus weakening the shot. The return with the left foot nearer the sideline allows your body and arm to work together for more power and accuracy.

When practicing the backhand, try hitting balls with both feet toward the net, sidestepping if necessary. From this position you will learn the feel of the shot better because you will have to turn your shoulders and hips. Remember that both hands are on the racket handle during the backswing, and the left hand is removed after it aids the right hand in the forward swing by a slight push. The pupil will learn that on the top-spin backhand drive, the back of the hand is more apt to be on top of the racket handle (one-quarter turn), while on the slice or the chop, the back of the hand can be more forward. This is a feeling, or a habit, that comes with practice.

Now we come to the advanced footwork, which should be used whenever time allows. This footwork has sometimes been branded as unorthodox, but it is hard to believe it deserves this name when and as it is used by the winners. Close analysis of tennis films at the USLTA Headquarters in New York reveals that this is indeed the footwork that made champions of Cochet, Borotra, Kramer, Tilden, LaCoste, Marble, Budge and others. The films indicate that the "almost" players are unconscious of this step and use it only 30% of the time instead of 90%.

Because we feel so strongly that this is the footwork for the beginner as well as the cham-

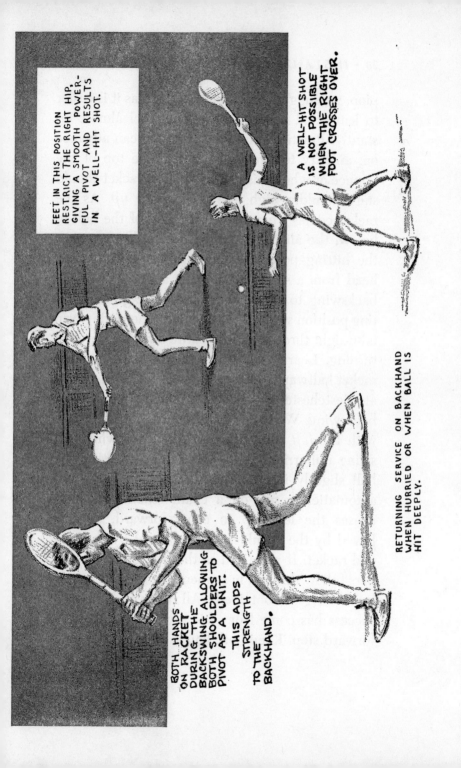

pion, we suggest that it be tried first, as it is easier to learn and it gives the correct feel almost instantly. Practice it on balls that you can advance on, and try to stroke the ball at the top of the bounce or when it is still rising. The racket should start shoulder high, the racket face *up*. As the racket comes from above the flight of the ball to below, the almost vertical racket face turns into the hitting position. This turning of the racket head from a string-up position at the end of the backswing to a perpendicular-to-the-ground hitting position speeds up the swing. The hitting arm is straight throughout the entire swing—the wrist turning. Learn to advance on the ball with the racket halfway back. This is what Sid Dufton, pro at Westchester Country Club, calls the two-part backswing. When the ball bounces, step forward with the *left* foot, complete the backswing and swing unhurriedly and smoothly, contacting the ball slightly in front of the left hip. This step automatically sets off a chain reaction that 1) causes the left hip to come forward, 2) followed by the shoulders, 3) followed by the arm and racket. If practiced so that these body members follow through in sequence, a smooth, effortless swing is obtained. All of my backhand success has come from this pivot, initiated by a forward step. Keep both hands on the racket and

THE MOST POWERFUL BACKHAND SHOT. THIS FORM ALLOWS
BETTER COURT COVERAGE THAN THE "CONVENTIONAL" RIGHT FOOT
FORWARD. SHOULD BE USED WHENEVER TIME ALLOWS.

ON ALL BACKHANDS
A SHORT INITIAL
FORWARD STEP
WITH THE LEFT
FOOT ADDS —
POWER
TO THE SHOT.

1.

2.

3.

KARL ROBERT RITTMANN

let go with the left hand only after the forward swing starts. This makes the shoulders move together and gives added strength to the shot.

Hit all balls waist high, or slightly below if necessary. If you should have to hit the ball at a higher point, hit it with the slice; that is, start the racket above the flight of the ball and finish, after the hit, below the ball. *On all high backhand slices, keep the elbow as low as possible and the racket head almost vertical.* Remember, the sliced backhand is hit with a one-quarter turn of the racket. Balls waist high or lower may be sliced, but they also may be top-spinned. For the latter, use the quarter-turn backhand grip, and start the racket head below the flight of the ball, finishing higher. This shot can be hit hard if you make sure the ball clears the net by a foot or two, for the top-spin will keep the ball in the court. *But remember, slice or drive, this shot is made with an initial step of the left foot.*

If the ball should come deep, and it is still on the rise when it reaches a spot slightly forward of the left hip, no forward step is made, and the shot is made with the left foot parallel to the right. Take a full backward and forward pivot, and follow through in the direction you wish the ball to take. On down-the-line shots, keep the racket on the ball as long as possible by keeping the racket on a path parallel to the sideline. The ball is taken a bit later than in a cross-court shot. Advancing the right foot slightly may make this pivot a bit easier for the beginner. Bending the knees on low balls will make the backswing more flexible. The knees are also used to add top-spin to the ball by unbending them as you come through. Dick Savitt, during the National Indoor Championships in 1961, used this knee action, with his feet pointing to the net, especially during return of service. But when you have time, get that left foot forward for extra power and control.

This footwork also helps to make your court covering much easier, because you are always in a good starting position for either backhand or forehand. Stepping across with the right foot (unless absolutely necessary) has the effect of two extra steps per shot, since you have to step back into the court to be in position for a forehand. Stepping over with the right foot also prevents a wind-up pivot and causes loss of power.

Summing up, there are three basic foot positions for the backhand:

1. Feet parallel or left foot advanced.
2. A step *forward* with the right foot. This step is made

immediately prior to the hit, but not until the backswing has been completed.

3. An initial step with the left foot forward or to the left prior to the hit, followed by a balance step with the right foot after the hit. The right foot lands *after* the ball has been hit.

4. When ball is far to the left, start by crossing over with the right foot, take a number of steps and land on the left foot. Be sure to start the backswing while traveling, and after a *full body pivot* swing forward.

Backhand check chart

1. Is the correct grip used?
2. Is the racket brought back with two hands?
3. Do shoulders, arm, and racket turn fully on the backswing?
4. Does the left foot step forward, initiating the swing, whenever possible?
5. Is the swing forward continuous, without pause from start to finish, and does it end when the arm can reach no further?
6. When time does not allow the initial step with the left foot, are balls hit with a full pivot, feet parallel and toes pointing to the net?
7. At all other times, does the right foot step *forward* *after* the backswing is completed?
8. Does the right foot cross over the left foot only when a wide reach is necessary?
9. Are close balls reached by sidestepping?
10. On sliced backhands does the racket start shoulder high, elbow low, racket face up (horizontal to the ground) and hit with a firm grip *at the top of the bounce*—the arm straight throughout?

6.
The forehand

There are three basic foot positions for the forehand drive:

1. Both feet parallel and toes pointing to the net or right foot advanced.
2. A variation of the above, stepping forward with the left foot *after* the backswing has been completed.
3. Stepping forward with the right foot prior to hitting the ball. The left foot comes forward for balance *after* the ball has left the racket. (This position should be learned first and used whenever possible.)
4. From position 1, step to the right with the left foot and after a few short steps land on the right and swing forward immediately after the right foot lands.

Be sure to take the racket at least half way back while approaching the ball.

The forehand grip is nothing more than shaking hands with the racket handle while the racket face is vertical to the ground.

Both flat shots and top-spin shots have their place in tennis. The flat shot is usually faster, because there is less spin to slow it down; but there is greater margin for error, since the ball travels in a straighter trajectory from its point of impact on the racket to the point where it hits the court. Unless the player is tall, or has developed exceptional skill, many flat shots will end frustratingly in the net. The top-spin shot, on the other hand, has less speed but is easier to control. While the spin slows the motion of the ball, it also gives it a curved trajectory through the air, clearing the net and falling into the opposite court with greater accuracy of placement.

In the forehand grip, the palm of the right hand is behind the handle when the racket face is vertical to the ground and the arm is extended, horizontal to the ground. Here again, it is impossible to use the V formed by the thumb and first finger as a guide to the proper grip. The popular theory is that this V of thumb and first finger should be on the top plane of the racket handle. But this guide can be used only in a general way, since palm sizes and finger lengths vary to a considerable degree. Placing the palm behind the handle and spreading the fingers comfortably around the grip will help the beginner to find his own correct hand position.

With this grip and the fingers of the left hand cradling the racket as it points toward the net, the player is in the ready position. Both feet should be pointing toward the net or in the general direction of the net posts. The player is slightly crouched, with knees slightly bent, and the weight forward, ready for action.

Now for the sequence of the actual forehand swing. Turn shoulders, right arm, and racket to the right in one compact movement, stopping when you feel this twisting motion tighten—or at five or six o'clock, if the net is considered twelve o'clock. *Do not move the left foot during the entire backswing.* The left foot rolls over to the outside of the big toe area, but does not leave the ground. This foot restricts the backswing and tightens the pivot or the "spring" in this twisting movement. Moving this foot during the backswing would loosen the "spring" and result in an armswing without the power of the body behind it, robbing it of its effectiveness. The racket may go back in a curved, elliptical motion, but care must be taken to see that this kind of backswing does not result in a loop.

When the "spring" has tightened—and *only then*—step *forward* toward the net with the left foot, toe to the net. At this point, you will notice that the right toe is pointing in the general direction of the right netpost—*not* parallel to the baseline. As soon as this forward step is taken—and it may be short—the shoulders, arm, and racket should start swinging forward to contact the ball at arm's length, waist high, and opposite the left toe. It should then continue forward until you can reach no further. The direction of the follow-through governs the direction the ball will take. The follow-through also allows the ball to remain in contact with the racket longer for greater accuracy. The forward stroke should be one continuous motion from start to finish, smooth and without jerkiness. The forward swing starts at a point below the ball and finishes high in the general area of the left shoulder. Contact the ball in the center of the racket.

For balls that come in to the right, sidestep or sideskip toward the right sideline, landing with the right foot nearer the sideline and the right toe pointing toward the netpost. If speed is needed to reach the ball in time, turn and run toward the sideline, but land on the right foot, with toe pointing toward the netpost, and then step forward with the left foot if time allows. If time does not allow, hit from this extended right foot position without a step forward with the left foot.

In receiving a particularly soft serve, stand inside the baseline and return it with both feet even with each other and the toes pointing toward the netposts. This toe position is most important, because it tightens the body pivot and allows the player to use a short backswing, which is helpful to accuracy.

If the player should find himself in a position with both feet pointing toward the right sideline, an arm shot should result, and power would have to be obtained for a forward lurch into the ball, instead of the smooth arm and body power emanating from the releasing of the "spring." The only way to generate power from this sideways position is by taking a long backswing, but this is a poor substitute, since by the time the ball is contacted, the swing is over. Also, from this sideways position, the ball can be seen only out of the corner of the eye, and accuracy naturally suffers. Only in an emergency, when the ball comes in far out to your right, is it permissible to step across with the left foot. The shot then

THE CORRECT FOREHAND FOOTWORK THE RIGHT FOOT FORWARD — THIS APPLIES TO ALL FOREHAND SHOTS EITHER RUNNING OR ROUTINE.

STROKING THE BALL FROM A SHORT BACKSWING AND SMOOTH PIVOT POSSIBLE ONLY FROM THIS FOOT POSITION.

1

2

KARL R. ZITTMANN

has to be a "touch" shot with the arm, practically devoid of the power of the body.

Now we come to the power forehand, which should be used whenever time allows. This employs footwork that is never shown when the player is asked to pose for the cameraman. It has always been considered unorthodox, but it has always been the foot position of the champions (though most of them do not know it and use the position instinctively rather than consciously).

Cochet used this footwork prior to hitting the return of service, as USLTA films clearly show. Under a picture of Cochet, *World Tennis* magazine says, "Cochet shows a disregard for conventional footwork"—! So then do Kramer, Tilden, LaCoste, Budge, and all the greats! If this is the unconventional footwork and the *winners* use it, I favor teaching it to all who wish to play better tennis.

When the ball bounces, and you wish to take it "on the rise" or at the "top of the bounce," step forward with the *right* foot, when the backswing has been completed, and contact the ball opposite the right hip. Get the feel of hitting at this spot, for it will prevent you from hitting too soon, or after the swing has been almost completed. *After* the ball has been contacted, you may step for-

—FOLLOW-THROUGH—
THE RIGHT FOOT
STEPS INTO THE
COURT AFTER
THE BALL IS
CONTACTED AND
RACKET FOLLOWS
THROUGH, DOWN
PAST THE LEFT
SIDE.

ward with the left foot for balance. On some shots it is not necessary to step forward with the left foot at all.

This footwork should be taught to beginners *first*, for it enables you to keep the ball on the racket longer, the backswing is shorter, and the follow-through longer, enhancing control and giving "feel" to the shot. It is the basis for the most powerful forehand stroke. The conventional sideways position, on the other hand, causes the player to contact the ball near the end of the swing, when its force is almost dissipated, and ends up in a short follow-through, defeating its own purpose.

Balls coming in to the right or to a point in front of the player should be reached with short steps while nearing the ball, followed by the longer right-foot step just prior to hitting it. This step automatically triggers a chain reaction that 1) allows the right hip to come through, 2) followed by the forward shoulder turn, 3) followed by the arm and racket. This "lag" of the right arm prior to the shoulder lead is the ingredient that makes for a smooth, ballistic swing.

When you know to which side the ball is coming, or when you are running for a ball, get the racket half-way back, and just before you approach the ball, finish the backswing and come forward unhurriedly. Many beginners (and advanced players, too) wait until they approach the ball before bringing the racket back. The result is a hurried swing that causes errors and jerkiness.

The backswing should be an elliptical movement. The elbow is kept waist-high on the backswing; the racket face may go shoulder-high, but do not lift the elbow to shoulder height, as some people suggest. Try to contact all balls at hip height or lower. This can be done by hitting the ball on the rise. There is nothing wrong in dropping the head of the racket on low balls, for it is impossible to hit some balls in any other way. However, bending the knees to hit low balls is essential, for it allows a level swing. Also, by unbending the knees at time of contact, more top-spin is put on a low ball, and the top-spin will keep the ball on the court when hit deeply.

Hit all balls so that they land between the service line and the baseline. By aiming for a spot one to two feet above the net, you'll make fewer errors. One cardinal rule that is almost too obvious to mention is *"Get the ball over the net!"* If you must make errors, make them by aiming at the baseline.

Forehand check chart

1. Is your grip correct?
2. Do shoulders and hips turn completely?
3. Is the racket brought back in an elliptical or horizontal plane and held at five or six o'clock?
4. Does the right foot come forward just prior to the hit whenever possible?
5. Are both feet parallel and pointing to the net on shots that must be hit hurriedly?
6. Does the left foot maintain contact with the ground during the entire backswing and step forward toward the net only after the backswing is completed on all other shots?
7. Do you contact the ball opposite the right hip with arm extended, and preferably at hip level?
8. Do you hit the ball in the center of the racket?

7.

The serve

In the past it has always been assumed that the serve was the most difficult stroke to learn. This is not so if it is broken down into its elements. It is the only shot that is not affected by the play of your opponent, who may, in other shots, put spins or skids on the ball or variations in its bounce.

Poise comes first. Stand motionless at the baseline, and don't let anyone hurry you. As in the ground strokes, the pivot is the basis here for smoothness and power. In order to learn the pivot early, the pupil should stand with the toes of both feet one inch behind and facing the baseline.

From this position it is practically impossible for a beginner to hit the serve without turning the shoulders, which is most important. If, later on, he feels that he is in better balance by moving the right foot back a few inches, he may do so. But the important thing at the beginning is to place the feet facing the net so that a pivot *has* to be made.

During the serve the backhand grip is used, or a grip that is in between a forehand and backhand grip. To learn the feel of the serve quickly, drop the head of the racket down your back; the butt end of the racket must be pointing toward the sky—straight up. This is very important, because without this position it is impossible to get the "feel" of the wrist action on the hit. As the left arm goes up to place the ball above the head, left palm facing the right sideline, turn the shoulders toward 6 o'clock (assuming the net to be 12 o'clock) and arch the back slightly. Turning the shoulders tightens the "spring" and allows the shoulders to spring back smoothly. As the shoulders uncoil, the elbow of the right arm, which was fully bent, starts to unbend. This unbending of the elbow allows the server to contact the ball on the upward and outward stroke. Too many beginners and advanced players do not get enough outward movement. This will put more spin on the ball

BALL PLACED WITH
SHOTPUT MOTION
DIRECTLY OVER-
HEAD.

RACKET BUTT
STRAIGHT UP.
FULL ELBOW
BEND.

and allow you to aim at a point higher above the net. The ball should be hit before it reaches the top of the left-hand toss. As the elbow unbends, the ball is contacted while the *wrist* is still cocked *above the head or to the left of it.* This action of the wrist causes the racket to contact the ball in a motion that is upward, definitely outward, then forward and over the top of the ball. Delaying this wrist action until the ball has been contacted is one of the main sources of power and control. First the elbow unbends, then the wrist uncocks, in sequence. The racket face is definitely parallel to the net at contact and during contact, it turns until it faces to the left. To feel the action, "throw" the racket head at the ball with a loose wrist and both feet close together. Keep feet planted while learning.

Swing the right foot over the baseline just prior to the hit. This foot helps bring the right hip forward and adds impetus to the shoulder turn. It also helps you to get in toward the net more quickly. Always let the right foot step into the court *after* the hit. Many servers are afraid of getting caught inside the baseline, for this area has always been considered as the danger zone; so they go to the other extreme by keeping both feet behind the baseline.

If your serve is hit correctly, you immediately

put the pressure on the receiver. Should his return be short, you have a good opportunity to move in, take it on the rise to score a placement, or force a weak return that may be volleyed for a winner from a strong net position.

Once the serve has been learned from the down-the-back position for rhythm, the racket may be started in a vertical position and then dropped down the back as the shoulders turn and the left hand places the ball above the head. With this abbreviated swing, it is a simple matter to hit the *rising* toss accurately in the center of the racket.

I have taught pupils to get the "feel" of this serve by emphasizing three points: 1) uncoil shoulders, 2) unbend elbow, 3) uncock wrist—all in sequence. Within three to five minutes, the rankest beginner should be able to see the pattern of the serve.

Sports Illustrated's book on tennis, with text by Talbert, shows Budge swinging the racket down and back, then up and forward. This is very difficult for a beginner to master, because Budge generally neglects the full elbow bend. (It is interesting to note that Gonzalez is now taking a shorter wind-up.) Not only does this book confuse the pupil, but the illustrations leave out the down-the-back position, and show the follow-through with the right foot behind the baseline. The book also suggests that the serve be hit 24 inches in front of the baseline! This may work—if you are 12 feet tall.

Other books tell you to contact the ball at the highest point you can reach. But the basis for real control is hitting the ball on the upward swing and definitely outward. This starts the ball up, and the spin causes it to drop into the opposite court. If your serve is not going in regularly, it is probably because you are not placing the ball correctly with the left arm, so that the right arm is not able to achieve a left-to-right motion or to contact the ball on the upward stroke. Remember that if the serve is not going in regularly, it is usually because you are not getting enough spin on the ball. Spin slows up the ball somewhat, but it makes the serve hard to return because it gives the ball a high hop and makes your opponent use a firm forward swing to keep the ball from flying off his racket.

Bouncing the ball on the court with the backhand grip will enable the pupil to learn the action of the wrist faster. Strike the ball at the beginning of the wrist snap, and allow the racket to go up and over the top of the ball. While learning, let the wrist flop slowly while in contact with the

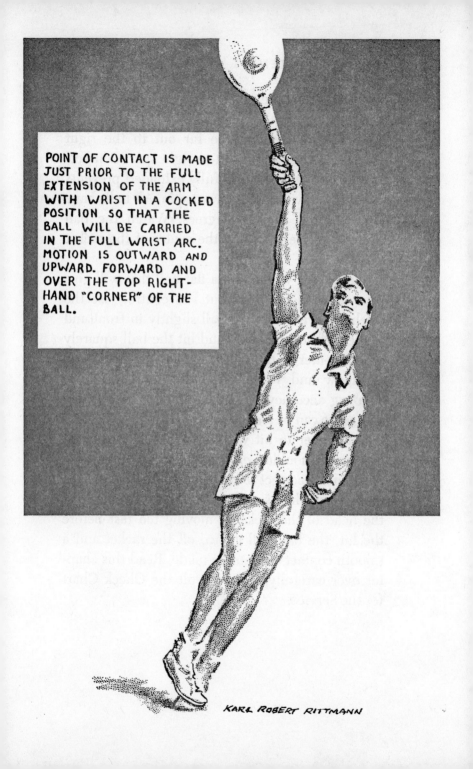

POINT OF CONTACT IS MADE
JUST PRIOR TO THE FULL
EXTENSION OF THE ARM
WITH WRIST IN A COCKED
POSITION SO THAT THE
BALL WILL BE CARRIED
IN THE FULL WRIST ARC.
MOTION IS OUTWARD AND
UPWARD. FORWARD AND
OVER THE TOP RIGHT-
HAND "CORNER" OF THE
BALL.

KARL ROBERT RITTMANN

ball. Don't start the snap before the ball has been contacted.

Contacting the ball too far out to the right prevents the use of the left-to-right spin. Contacting the ball with the arm fully extended prevents the use of upward, or forward spin. All balls have some spin in varying degrees. Watch the ball closely and feel it hitting the center of the racket strings.

Should you wish to hit a flat ball that will give your serve more speed but less control, use the forehand grip. Toss the ball slightly in front and to the right of the head, and hit the ball squarely on the center of the racket with a complete bend of elbow and wrist. With this short wind-up, amazing accuracy can be obtained, although the spin serve can be angled more sharply.

Remember to hit with a slow, lazy motion at first, with shoulder, elbow, and wrist falling into place in the correct sequence. Feel the ball on the racket, and then speed up the follow-through. If the head of the racket is moving too fast before the hit, the ball will glance off the racket and a smooth contact will not be made. Read this chapter over carefully, then consult the Check Chart for the Service.

Service check chart

1. Are you using the backhand grip?
2. Are both feet one inch from the baseline?
3. Do the shoulders turn completely to right and left?
4. Is the ball released with the left arm fully extended, palm facing toward the right sideline?
5. Is the ball placed above the head so that the racket may swing forward from the left of the ball to the right of it?
6. Is it contacted while on the *upward* toss?
7. Is the ball hit in the middle of the racket face in the upswing?
8. Does the right elbow bend completely?
9. Is the ball contacted at the beginning of the wrist snap?
10. Does the racket go upward, outward, and over the ball?
11. Does the right foot swing forward just before the hit and step into the court *after* the ball is contacted?
12. Does the racket finish its stroke on the left side of the body?
13. Is the ball hit with a slow, lazy motion, with all elements working in sequence?

8.
The volley

The volley is like the boxer's jab; it is the easiest stroke of all, because generally it involves only the wrist and the forearm. All volleys are hit from above the line of flight of the ball well out in front, so that both eyes can be kept on the ball. The feet do not move except in a side-stepping motion. It is necessary to step over with either foot into a sideways position only on impossible "gets" or when you know the ball is not coming back.

The volley is hit with two motions: 1) get the racket above the line of flight of the ball, 2) punch it forward, downward, and under or around to the right side of the ball. Keep the racket above the wrist so that wrist action can help you to angle it or add power to the punch. Use a short pivot, especially on backhand volleys.

If you have to move in to volley a soft return, step forward with the right foot for the forehand (reverse the feet for the backhand). Use two hands on the racket in a backhand volley (see chapter on the Backhand). Keep facing the net as much as possible, and get sideways only if you have to reach fast to far right or left. Beveling the racket face up will enable you to get the low volleys; angling it to the right or left will enable you to angle the balls off.

Some volleys can be simply blocked. To hit a volley that drops dead after clearing the net, hit with a loose wrist. On backhand volleys, place the thumb up the back of the racket handle for better support. Full volleys are hit in the air with the same motion as the forehand drive. Keep the racket high when awaiting a volley. *The best place to practice the volley is on the service line.* This makes you flatten out your volleys and is the best way to learn the right racket angle.

The full volley is hit like a forehand drive with a short backswing and some top spin.

Alice Marble Hits a Forehand

Bruce Barnes Hits a Forehand

Budge Patty Hits a Forehand

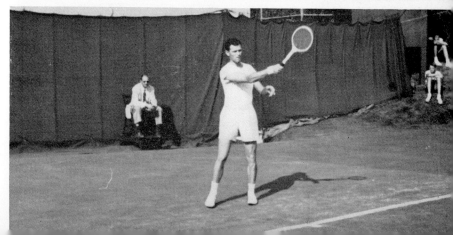

Herbert Flam Hits a Backhand

Lew Hoad Backhand Volley

This stroke-volley is executed four or five feet in front of the service line. It's a below-waist shot handled more like a stroke than a volley. Hoad's backswing and follow-through are unusually big and while he gets tremendous depth and speed, he must make more errors—since he's almost driving a ball from below-net level and close to the barrier. It's amazing he makes so many winners as he does considering the fact he allows himself so little margin for error.

Dick Savitt Serves

Sidney Wood Hits a Backhand

Al Cantello Throws the Javelin

(courtesy *Scholastic Coach*)

THE PUNCH VOLLEY,
EMPOLYING THE
SHORTENED PIVOT.
NOTE POSITION OF
FEET POINTING TOWARD
NET. WHEN TIME ALLOWS,
LEFT FOOT SHOULD
BE ADVANCED.

Volley check chart

1. Is the racket placed above the line of flight of the ball?
2. Is the ball contacted well forward, with wrist action going from above the line of flight of the ball downward?
3. Do the toes remain pointed toward the net?
4. Do the feet move only in a sidestepping manner and cross over each other only when the ball is too wide to handle any other way?
5. When you have to move forward for a forehand volley, do you hit with the right foot forward (left foot on a backhand volley)?
6. Is the racket beveled up on low balls?

9.

The auxiliary strokes

On chops, slices, lobs, and drop shots, the footwork is still the same as it is for the top-spin drives. The only difference is in the path of the racket.

For the slice, this path starts above the flight of the ball and turns around the right side of the ball and underneath. The higher the ball is, the more the stroke approaches the slice service, where the racket goes over the top of the ball before heading downward in the follow-through. The racket is held in a vertical position.

For the chop, the racket is horizontal and goes down and under the ball.

The drop shot is similar, except that the wrist collapses as the ball is contacted. Let the wrist become floppy at the moment of impact, and be sure that the ball just clears the net. Too many drop shots end up as outright gifts to the opponent because they fail to clear the net. Contacting the ball on the rise adds extra back-spin to the ball and makes it more difficult for your opponent to retrieve it. Should he catch it on the top of the bounce, he is in a good position to put it away on you. All drop shots should have the element of surprise—don't overwork a good thing.

Backhand drop shots are easier to disguise, because many backhands used by the average player are undercut to begin with, which means that the racket starts above the flight of the ball, and the only added touch necessary is to soften the shot with a loose wrist.

The overhead, or smash, is the stroke used to return a lob. It employs the same technique as the serve, but the player is closer to the net and in a better position to put the ball away.

As soon as you are aware that a lob is being hit to you, get your racket down your back, point your left hand at the ball and keep it there, using it as a guide toward the spot where the racket must hit the ball. Generally, you must hit the ball from left to right. Racket is almost horizontal above the head at contact point and then goes up and out and downward. Be sure to keep facing the net just before you contact the ball. If possible, advance the right foot prior to hitting the ball.

Do not attempt to put away a deep ball from behind your head; the only thing to do with such a ball is to play it back as safely as you can and wait for another one that you can hit in front of you or just above your head. Remember, don't try for an angled overhead unless you can put it away.

The lob is used when passing seems inadvisable. Lobs also should be employed when you are caught off the court and need the time to get back into position. High and deep to the backhand corner is the best spot at such a time.

Lobs are good for purposes of surprise or variation in strategy. If you have been passing the net-rusher or dipping wide angles to his feet, a lob will keep him from coming in close. One lob shot that is not used often enough is similar to a slow passing shot on the backhand side, high enough so that the net man has to reach backhanded above his shoulder, and wide enough so that he cannot reach it as he could if the ball were lower.

Some lobs are top-spun so that they just clear the net-man's extended reach and bounce away from him, making it impossible for him to retrieve them. Remember, hit a lob deep and high when you are in a hole.

To return service with a lob is difficult, since the spin on the ball calls for a firmer follow-through so that the ball does not fly off the face of the racket. The lob is effective only when judiciously used in conjunction with drives and soft angles.

The half-volley is hit with the same motion as the drive, with the single difference that it is hit three or four inches off the ground, the bounce and the hit only a few inches apart. This is a much easier shot to stroke than some believe. If you practice and you can hit the ball on the center of the racket, the results are amazing. It is when you have to hit a ball that travels about a foot or two from the bounce to the hit that timing has to be delicate. These balls have to be watched very carefully, but when hit with proficiency, they will get you out of tight spots and possibly give you an advantage because the return is unexpected.

In the half-volley, get your head down close to the ball, hit with a short backswing, and watch the ball hit the strings of the racket. A quick, last-minute adjustment of the racket face will get you out of difficulty if you concentrate.

A STRATEGICALLY PLACED LOB TO THE BACKHAND CORNER.

10.

How to watch the ball

Most of the books on tennis instruct the reader to watch the ball hit the racket, but all the eye doctors I have questioned about it claim that this can't be done without taking your eye *off* the ball. The eye, they explain, does not see the ball continuously, but focuses on it in little jumps.

When the ball gets to the nearest spot where your eyes focus most clearly, bring your racket through smoothly and confidently and hit the ball at this spot. Photos of top stars show that they look *up* when watching the ball clearly is no longer possible. Experience will let you "feel" the center of the racket without looking at it.

When the ball is coming at you from over the net, concentrate only on its general direction; but as soon as it bounces, then it is time to *start focusing* on it, so that you can try to hit it at the top of the bounce. Watching for this top of the bounce, incidentally, automatically forces you to watch the ball closely.

The footwork taught in this book allows both eyes to watch the ball in a relaxed manner, whereas the sideways stance recommended by the others forces you into a position where all you can do is peek at it out of the corner of one eye (the *wrong* eye, by the way, if you are going to watch the ball hit the center of the racket, as they urge you to do—just try it!).

When you have become moderately proficient at the game, stand in on the ball and hit it on the rise. This takes greater eye concentration, but the added momentum of a faster ball gives you more speed with less effort. However, if the court is giving the ball bad bounces, don't try to hit it on the rise, but give it a longer look to make very sure of its final direction.

11.

Strategy

In Singles

Strategy is nothing more than a plan of action designed to place the ball out of the reach of your opponent. It may take several shots to achieve this, but it is best to have a plan behind every shot. The serve generally starts the strategy and should give you the advantage to begin with, and only by a strong counter strategy can your opponent take the play away from you.

Since your serve is the starting point of your strategy, give it careful attention. Always get the serve over the net—if you are going to miss it, miss it beyond the service line, because a short serve will only get you into trouble. Your only excuse for hitting a serve into the net is an attempt at a sharp angle, where the area you are aiming for is small and the margin of error not very great.

The next thing to concentrate on, relative to your serve, is placement. While serves to the backhand are generally considered best and are used about 85% of the time, a short, unexpected, angled serve to the forehand that pulls the receiver off the court can be very effective. If you can keep this shot low, below the level of the net, the receiver most likely will not be able to put the ball away. You are then in a very good spot to hit deep to his backhand corner and keep the pressure on. But a word of warning: should this angled serve bounce too high and give the receiver time to get set for it, his hard drive cross-court or down the line may get you in trouble when the advantage should have been yours.

Modern tennis demands that you reach the net before your opponent, but when you are the receiver, it requires at least two shots before you can firmly establish yourself at the net against a good serve. Return all serves that are not followed at the net deep to your opponent's baseline, preferably on his backhand side. Should he be a top-flight player and follow his serve to the net, dipping the ball to his feet will make him play upward and prevent him from putting the shot away. Or you can pass him outright on his backhand side, or try the angle to his forehand. Should none of these maneuvers work, it might be well to place a lob over his head and to the backhand side—high enough to get over his head but not so high as to enable him to run back and smash it away while it is still in the air. The most strategic lob is one that goes to your opponent's backhand and causes him to take the ball on a bounce.

When advancing to the net, always cover and protect against the possibility of a straight-ball return; for they are the fastest, while the angled balls are slow and dippy. Straight balls are hit hard, while angles have to be heavily "topped" with spin, which slows them down somewhat. Take a piece of paper and figure out the angles at which the ball may be returned and still be in the court, and then decide how to cover them.

One plan of strategy is to try to maneuver your opponent from corner to corner; or hit a short angle followed by a deep shot to the opposite side of the court—or back to the same spot, if he appears to be moving too quickly to his opposite corner. Playing a ball to your opponent's strength, which might be the forehand, can enable you to hit the next ball to his weakness, which might be the backhand.

A well-sliced low shot deep to the backhand is much better than a high-bouncing drive, for it causes your opponent to hit upward. Also, this same shot played deep and straight at your opponent's feet will make him hit from a cramped position so that he cannot stroke the ball at arm's length. Don't underrate this shot, especially on your serve.

A popular misconception about strategy that has appeared frequently in previous tennis books is the theory of the "danger zone." This area, between the baseline and service line, has always been considered No Man's Land, and the reader is warned always to hit from behind the baseline or pass through this "danger zone" and volley between the service line and the net. Admittedly, it is more difficult to play a ball bouncing near the baseline, but there are, nevertheless, times when you should be inside the baseline. On return of serve, for instance, you are in a better position to cut down the possibility of a sharply angled, off-the-court serve. Also, after you have served, it is often wise to step into the court, about one foot inside the baseline or nearer, depending on the severity of your serve. From this position you are in an excellent spot to advance on a ball that is returned short, and you will be able to hit the ball on the rise or at the top of the bounce to an unprotected area of the opponent's court and then advance to the net. Furthermore, from this position inside the baseline, you may also be able to volley the return of service. Playing behind the baseline makes it necessary for you to hit too many balls ankle high, and all your shots will have to travel upward. In addition, sustained behind-the-line play may change you into a retriever, and the psychology of play then becomes one of timidity. You must think positively about all shots, for confidence leads to success.

We have mentioned the strategy of angling the ball and the strategy of varying the height of the ball. Another device is to vary the speed of the ball. Generally speaking, don't hit a hard drive unless you are aiming for an exposed part of the court, or the speed may cause trouble. For a fast ball hit within easy reach of your opponent may come back at you faster than it was hit. If you are caught off the court, a slowly-hit top-spin drive will give you time to get back into position; but if you return it fast, it will leave you vulnerable to a harder-hit return to the opposite side of the court.

So remember, there is a time to hit hard, a time to hit softly, a time to lob, a time to hit low, a time to hit high, and a time to angle. All shots have their place at specific times. Tennis is a game of the head, so watch the champions to discover the sequence of their shots. Also, watch your opponent's game when he is playing against someone else. What are his strong strokes? What are his weaknesses? Close analysis of his game will make all your strokes more effective against him.

In Doubles

Strategy in doubles presents the same basic angles to contend with as in singles, but here you have a partner to help or hinder you. Before playing doubles, you and your partner should agree on a plan of action. To play otherwise can make the best player look ridiculous, because his partner is nullifying his own good position play.

When you are returning service, your partner should always play parallel with you, unless you intend to follow your return to the net. Then you are parallel to your partner at the net, which is the best place to be. However, if you are up against a good serve, stay back and wait before you both try to take the net position. Sometimes your partner can stand halfway up to the net and drop back fast if he sees that you are having trouble returning the service. Always play parallel and move together sideways.

When you are serving, protect your partner by serving to the backhand side of the forehand court. This will enable him to play more to the middle of the service and poach on the return. Should you serve wide—that is, to the extreme side of the service court—your partner must immediately guard against the straight alley shot, leaving you to cover the wide gap which will then separate your team, unless you wish to ignore the possibility of an angle. Return all balls as nearly as possible to the center of the court, and use the angle shot when you are putting the ball away or when you are using a soft angled dipping shot. If your opponents are hugging the baseline, play the ball deep and come into the net for a volley or overhead smash.

About 80 to 90% of your first serves to the forehand court should be hit to the backhand side of that court; and 70% of serves to the backhand court should also be hit to the backhand side. When serving into the backhand service court, try not to hit too wide an angle, as this takes your partner out of the play because he has to protect his alley.

Any player who has developed control of his serve should hit well over the net and have the ball land near the service line. Keep the serve deep, at a speed that will enable you to get in to the net behind it.

A good rule of doubles play is to cover the straight shot on your side of the court, and keep as nearly parallel with your partner at all times as possible. Balls hit down the middle may be taken by the stronger player. Or, if the players are about equal, a safe rule to follow is for the one who hit the last ball to take the return when it is down the middle. But this rule applies only when both partners are playing side by side. If one man is at the net, he should handle all balls within reach.

If you have an unbalanced team, there are ways to protect the weaker player. When the weak partner is serving into the "ad" or backhand court, the stronger partner may play what is sometimes called the "B" formation—that is, he takes his position at the left side of the net. All the returns that get by him will be hit to the weaker player's forehand, which is generally his stronger shot. Also, if you are playing with a weak partner, place him close to the net when you are receiving service. Your return must be hit hard or be well-placed. Should the other team gamble by hitting to your weak partner at the net, all he has to do is hold up his racket and angle the ball for a placement—the easiest shot in the game.

12.

Equipment

Stringing

For a long time, I would have nothing to do with nylon stringing; the most expensive gut was all I would use. When the smooth nylon came out, I tried it but found that many balls landed in the bottom of the net, especially low balls with the necessary top-spin. Because I was using the wrong footwork at the time (that being taught in all the books), I found that my arm swing traveled too fast for a smooth contact with the ball. This would result in a glancing blow, and the ball would skid off the racket. Also, in keeping with the theory that all rackets must be strung tight, I had the nylon strung that way. This made the smooth surface even more slippery, and I gave up on nylon with the feeling that it would never attain the efficiency of gut.

But recently, at the insistence of Bob Crandall, I tried his new Vantage nylon and was pleasantly surprised; for here at last was a thin-gauge stringing, unaffected by moisture and long-wearing, which plays so close to gut that you have to be almost neurotic to see the difference.

Vantage, according to the specifications, was manufactured to perform at 60-pound stringing, a poundage that gives excellent control with plenty of zing. And now, with the smooth swing obtained by the footwork recommended in this book, Vantage makes the game economical. Even if you can afford to pay more for gut, remember that nylon at around 60 pounds may help your game and is an all-weather string.

Balls

To play with tennis balls that have lost their nap changes the whole concept of the game. Light balls float and require a great deal of top-spin to keep them in the court. Slices have to be played close to the net; otherwise these shots will tend to sail beyond the baseline.

But with the advent of no-compression balls from Sweden, this floating tendency has been greatly minimized, and balls are no longer the expensive problem that they once were. These new balls remain uniform in their bounce, have a very substantial wool-dacron cover, and remain heavy longer than the compression-type balls, which have a tendency to lose their compression eventually, even when the cover is still in good shape.

Furthermore, the new no-compression balls may be cleaned when they get black from play on asphalt or dirt courts. Just throw them in the washing machine with a touch of bleach, and they come out snow-white and with the nap fluffed up. Not only is their visibility back to standard, but the fluffing revives the nap so that their bounce is more up-and-down, instead of low and skidding like an airplane landing at LaGuardia.

Rackets

Because most of the rackets on the market today are made by a variety of manufacturers, even though they bear similar brand names, it is not practical to choose a racket because of its label. The important thing to look for is the grade of wood in the frame. After you have decided that the wood in the racket of your choice is the best, count the laminations in the head. In a quality racket, there should be around eight or nine of them.

Other important features in a racket are the spacing of the holes around the frame, whether paint has been used to cover up cheap workmanship, and the quality of the material used in the leather grip.

Rackets should weigh in the vicinity of 13 to 15 ounces. Use the heaviest racket you can control at the net, and if you are not sure of one racket, try several of different weights until you find one that is right. I suggest trying them at the net, or serving, because that is where quick racket work is essential, and if you can get the racket on the majority of volleys hit to you, you can assume that the racket is right for you.

The weight of the racket should be slightly in the head. The balance point should be 13½ inches from the end of the racket handle. To determine where the weight is, balance the racket on a knife edge. If the length of the racket is 27 inches, the even balance point will be 13½ inches from the butt.

Handles should be big enough to allow a space of about ½ inch between little finger and heel of the palm. All of the inside of the palm and all of the fingers should come in contact with the handle for good gripping, but the fingers should not overlap.

Shoes

Few people realize how important it is to wear tennis shoes that do not slip during stroking. On the forehand, the important foot is the right one, and on the backhand it is the left. If either foot moves during the backswing, it changes the length of the backswing. Even a slight change in the angle of the foot because of slipping during the backswing makes a difference of four to six inches in the length of the swing. Championship players often compensate for this by their years of experience on the court, but why handicap yourself needlessly.

On good clay courts, the caretakers usually allow only smooth soles of the newer design with "squeegee" action. While some cleated sneakers will also give you good traction, they dig up the courts, and at many clubs they have been outlawed.

Equipment unwisely selected can be expensive and can actually hinder, rather than help, your proficiency in the game. So pay close attention to the features pointed out in this chapter, and you will find that you can play better tennis at a minimum cost. New products are coming out on the market, as well as new refinements of older products, and there is no reason why tennis should put a strain on anyone's pocketbook if he selects his equipment sensibly.

13.
The ball trap

All jobs are divided into three parts: get ready, do the job, and clean up.

For a long time it has been apparent to motion economists that time has been wasted in connection with almost every type of work.

We are concerned at this time with clean-up, because if this is done correctly, the get-ready also will be taken care of automatically. The average tennis pro picks up in an eight-hour day about six thousand tennis balls. This costs money. An expensive waste of time, an expensive waste of the pupil's money, and nothing added to the lesson but hard work! Some people believe we should leave this ball-picking drudgery in the lesson—they claim it is good exercise. But if it is, the pupil does not need a teacher to learn this form of exercise; and if it isn't, the time can more profitably be used in hitting balls.

With this deplorable waste of time, money, and energy in mind, the author has invented a Ball Trap to eliminate needless drudgery, thus making tennis lessons more efficient, and playing more pleasurable. This mechanical device is simple in design, and works on a ramp, net, and trough principle, following the principle of gravity for drop delivery as used in industry. It comes in twelve-foot folding sections and is readily assembled on the court in five minutes. Individual sections may be used for practice, or the Trap may be extended to cover the whole width of the court for group lessons or for playing.

Placed behind the baseline, the Ball Trap catches 95% or more of all balls hit and returns them to a central spot for re-use. New patterns of pupil placement on the court can be achieved with the use of this Trap, as will become apparent the first day it is used, for all pupils can be hitting balls at the same time, thereby increasing the learning span for everyone. The Ball Trap may also be used in conjunction with an automatic ball-throwing machine. By reloading the ball thrower from the Trap, you maintain a continuous conveyor system. All balls are "untouched by human hand," except in actual play. And actual play is where the fun is, and that's where it ought to be kept.

14.

Pros and cons

Mis-takes from other books

The following pearls of unwisdom are bits of advice to be found in some of the other books on tennis. I have read them all carefully and tried them out on the court. All my years of mediocre playing were based on them, because I believed them to be gospel. Over recent years, however, careful analysis of the game, research in numberless clinics, and close observation of big name players in action have convinced me that the authors of these books don't take their own advice when they are playing to win. Hence, why should I—or you?

Here are some of them:

BUDGE: "You want to stand sideways to the flight of the ball."

DOEG: "One cardinal rule is that you must stand sideways to the net."

MACE: "A baseball batter stands sideways to the plate. In tennis we create an imaginary plate by standing sideways."

TILDEN: "You must hit the ball opposite your belt buckle."

SEDGEMAN: "You hit the ball with the arm fully extended on the serve."

BUDGE: "When you volley, get sideways."

BUDGE (LLOYD): "You must turn your back to the ball on the backhand and look over your right shoulder."

BUDGE (LLOYD): "The hitter should get in as long a stroke as possible before meeting the ball at that point (i.e., in front of the left leg)."

BEASLEY: "On the forehand. From your ready position, with your racket back, take one step forward with your left foot. Maintaining this sideways position, advance toward the ball."

TILDEN: "From a point about shoulder-high, toss the ball to a point as high as the racquet will comfortably reach."

EARL BUCHOLTZ: "Freeze the body and swing just the arm for better control."

KRAMER: "Every stroke is made with your body sideways to the net. This allows you freedom of swing that puts accuracy and speed in your shots. You never saw a baseball player who stepped to the plate and faced the pitcher, or a golfer who faced the fairway."

Sports Illustrated Magazine: "On the forehand, contact the ball 18 inches forward of the left foot" (when standing sideways!). Also, "Contact the serve 24 inches in front of the baseline" (with the right foot still behind the baseline!).

THE USLTA TEACHING FILM: Considerable yardage of film shows the USLTA-recommended method of teaching and is followed by clips of Maria Bueno and Darlene Hard playing in the finals of the National Championships. The announcer in the film invites us to note how these champions use the principles just seen in the teaching half of the film; but close observation shows that the two best women players in the world do just the opposite! For example, where the USLTA recommends standing sideways with left foot advanced, these champions face the net and advance the right foot. As Wes Gaffer of the New York *Daily News* remarked, "The film contradicts almost every phase of the organization's teaching programs, which are hilariously included in the film."

These are only a few of the shibboleths of the great—the list could run into pages. But the one point they all emphasize is that the footwork of the champions should not be attempted by beginners. But how do beginners learn this footwork if they don't try it? And who says beginners are not capable of correct footwork, even if their control is off target at first? Frank Gilbreth said, "Teach the right method at standard speed, and the results will take care of themselves." We should never teach a position that later has to be discarded.

And Now, "Well Done"

Now that I have quoted what I believe to be wrong in other books, I must mention what I believe to be right in them.

Tilden's comments on the center theory are excellent. He was a great strategist and delved deeply into the mystical world of the psychology of play. He was also an individualist, often criticized for his eccentricities. Once during a match that he was losing, the committee of the United States Lawn Tennis Asociation, none of whose members ever reached his stature, said to him, "The committee feels you should go to the net more." Happily, Tilden *was* an individualist and didn't pay too much attention to committees.

Bob Harmon's *Use Your Head in Tennis* is written in an easy style and contains much that is original. Unfortunately, while he admits that Kramer hits the ball with his toes to the net, he *apologizes* for it and says that when you have time, you should stand sideways. Nevertheless, much hard work went into his book, and there is a great deal in it that is worthwhile if you will overlook his ideas about footwork.

Talbert's book on doubles shows a multitude of plays and is probably the most thorough study of doubles play that has appeared in print. Even though Billy *always* advances his right foot on the forehand himself, he advises his readers to do the opposite in the *Sports Illustrated Book of Tennis*. The beautifully drawn illustrations of Budge cannot save this book from utterly distorting the mechanics of the strokes. However, this is one of the first books to reveal the signals used by the champions.

Sarah Palfrey Cooke's book, *Winning Tennis,* has flip-over pages that show all the strokes in motion-picture action. This format might have produced one of the best books ever written on tennis, if it were not for the "posed" footwork.

Tom Stowe, writing in *World Tennis,* says of his star pupil, Don Budge, "This shows an old weakness of his . . . allowing his left hand to come too far out." It is only because Budge is *posing,* arbitrarily, in the sideways position that Stowe recommends that his left hand come out for balance. All the old films of Budge reveal that this has never been a weakness of his. Furthermore, the 1938 championship pictures show that Budge never used the forehand sideways stance, except on rare occasions and then only *after* the ball had left his racket. This is not the best position from a court-covering standpoint, for when Budge crosses over with his left foot, he has to cross back to put himself into position for the next shot. But Don's natural athletic ability compensated for his faulty footwork. One can't help wondering how much greater Budge might have been had he *know*n the secret of correct footwork!

Many Thanks

Even though I have discussed my theory with Budge, Kramer, Cooke, Riggs, Segura, Gonzalez, Talbert, the United States Lawn Tennis Association, the Professional Lawn Tennis Association, *World Tennis* Magazine, the New England Lawn Tennis Association, the Providence *Journal* School of Tennis, and the Rhode Island Tennis Organization, none of them has ever had enough curiosity, to date, to come out to the tennis court to see the theory in action! Notable exceptions to this amazing lack of intellectual curiosity in the area of their own professed greatest love are Harry Twist, pro at the American Yacht Club; Jack Johnson, Covaleigh Club, both at Rye, N.Y., and John Dunn from Hemptstead, Long Island. John Dunn has been teaching much of the footwork I advocated for years and has some real champions coming along.

Herman Fagel, at Miami Shores, is a dedicated pro who has introduced tennis into the grade schools.

Mercer Beasley, at the age of 78, invited me to his summer camp to run a clinic. Even though he knew that my system differed from his, he said, "Don't let anyone say that Beasley ever stopped learning." He is an idea man that we can all learn from; I never visit his apartment at Forest Hills that he doesn't give me some good advice.

Bobby Riggs has been a good friend, and while he has never completely endorsed my system (although he can't explain why he won't, except

THE FOOTWORK USED BY THE CHAMPIONS, NOT THE LOSERS, ARE SHOWN ON THESE PAGES.

FREE-FLOWING FOLLOW-THROUGH THE RESULT OF A FULL BALLISTIC PIVOT.

CONTACT ON RUNNING SHOT. RIGHT FOOT POINTING TOWARD NET. LEFT FOOT LANDS AFTER BALL LEAVES RACKET.

4

3

on grounds of not wanting to hurt his *other* friends in tennis), he has been most helpful in many ways. Bobby plays natural and instinctively beautiful tennis and never had to listen to any teacher (perhaps this explains his lack of interest in objective analysis). He has a rare ability to concentrate even when there is confusion all around him. These days, he plays tennis just for the joy of it (with a wager thrown in to make it more interesting), and gracefully accepts the fact that his days of great play are behind him. However, when open tennis becomes a reality, Bobby will be back in there, fighting in the senior ranks. I'm sure we would all like to see him compete again.

With Sid Dufton, pro at Westchester Country Club, I have had several interesting conversations, and Sid was kind enough to allow me to make a teaching film at his club. He is the originator of the circular backboard and other innovations that could, if more widely publicized, result in greater interest in and better instruction of tennis. A great teacher who places sportsmanship first and always commands the greatest respect from his pupils, Sid has our best wishes in his latest endeavor, which is medical research, where his open-mindedness should carry him far.

There are many others who have been helpful,

such as the staff members at the many camps I have visited, where I was invited to teach a system contrary to all their traditions and where the coaches, with a fine display of professional generosity and receptiveness, were eager to learn, discuss, and exchange ideas and techniques. Every time I taught, I learned something, and my summer camp tour was as instructive as it was enjoyable.

But the best way to settle this controversy about the teaching of tennis, as in any other controversy, is to exchange ideas freely and then let the public in as judge. The reader is therefore invited to try these theories for himself on the court; he is also urged to remember that learning the game correctly right from the start will enhance his enjoyment of it in years to come. For there is no greater frustration than to spend twenty years in the practice of a technique only to learn, the day after you have given away your racket in despair, that the still, small voice inside you that kept whispering, "something is wrong," was right—and that it was the teacher who was wrong. So be as careful of the soundness of the theories you employ as you are of the equipment you purchase. Make sure of the heroes you put on that pedestal before you emulate them; play a little each day; enjoy it; and live twenty years longer. Tennis, played right, is good for your disposition.

The Things That Happen!

Some tennis players claim they play for fun only and are not interested in changing their game for the sake of improvement. One tournament player told me that he didn't expect to win his match but was just going to have some fun. During the match, however, an elderly lady who was watching said to me, "Who is that fellow throwing his racket against the backstop after every point?"

"Oh," I replied, looking at my friend's exhibitions of frustration, "he's a racket-tester from one of the big racket manufacturers. He's out for some fun."

Those who will not learn how to improve their game always insist they don't take the game seriously. Naturally—how could they? This would be easier to believe if they gave up the game or stopped keeping score—or at least didn't visibly lose their tempers over every lost match.

Many players who have been playing the game for years with poor results have told me, "You can't teach an old dog new tricks." But this is not

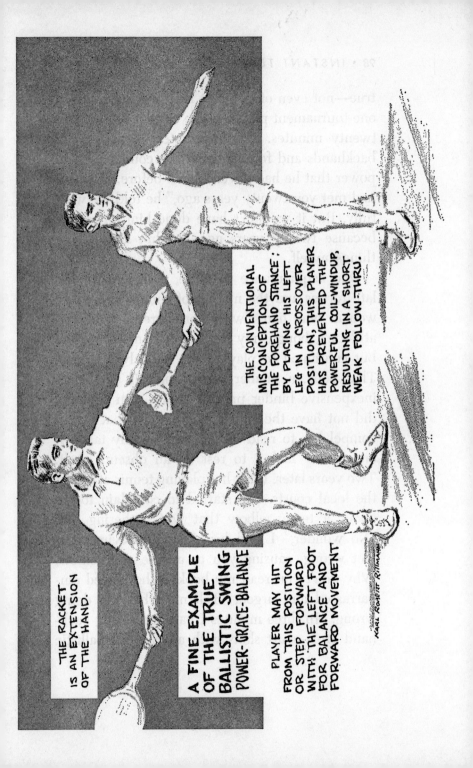

THE RACKET IS AN EXTENSION OF THE HAND.

A FINE EXAMPLE OF THE TRUE BALLISTIC SWING POWER-GRACE-BALANCE

PLAYER MAY HIT FROM THIS POSITION OR STEP FORWARD WITH THE LEFT FOOT FOR BALANCE AND FORWARD MOVEMENT

THE CONVENTIONAL MISCONCEPTION OF THE FOREHAND STANCE: BY PLACING HIS LEFT LEG IN A CROSSOVER POSITION, THIS PLAYER HAS PREVENTED THE POWERFUL COIL-WINDUP, RESULTING IN A SHORT WEAK FOLLOW-THRU.

KARL ROBERT RITHMAN

true—not even of dogs. At Longwood I changed one tournament player to the correct footwork in twenty minutes. He immediately began to hit backhands and forehands with a confidence and power that he had never known before. "I wish I had met you twenty years ago," he told me wistfully. But it wouldn't have done him any good, because twenty years ago I didn't know these things myself.

One acquaintance of mine, a woman in her late forties and the mother of three children (a woman who had always considered herself unathletic), bought my early book some time ago, but continued to play as she had always done. That book, a smaller version of this one in an inexpensive binder printed at my own expense, did not have the claims to greatness that would compel her to read it; she had politely taken it and gently laid it to rest on an obscure shelf. Two years later, I saw her playing tennis at one of the local courts. She started to complain to me about a tennis elbow that was bothering her. "No wonder," I told her. "You're moving your feet wrong, causing you to misuse your elbow. Why don't you read my book?" She looked embarrassed and urged, "Tell me what I'm doing wrong." In three minutes I had her hitting backhand cross-court shots with a beautiful ballistic swing. In amazement she said, "I didn't realize how easy this game was!" The next time I saw her, she remarked, "The trouble with your system is, I'm winning all my matches too easily, I don't get enough exercise!" She has had to look for tougher competition.

I once taught the captain of the Rhode Island Reds hockey team how to play tennis. For a gag, we staged it on television on ice, wearing skates. Because the skates prevented him from using the classic sideways stance, the hockey captain immediately started to hit with a beautiful ballistic motion. If your game is off, try pointing your feet at the net (you don't necessarily have to wear skates). Incidentally, in pony polo, the player makes his best shots with his feet pointing toward goal; even if he could *make* the pony stand sideways in the "classic stance," I doubt if it would improve his game!

Seriously, I have seen too many intelligent and well-coordinated youngsters going through the agonies inflicted on them by poor teaching. And I have seen their faces light up when I have pointed out to them that they were swinging unnaturally, against the laws of nature, against what their own sound instinct would tell them to do. And I have heard them exclaim, when I showed them the right way, "This *feels so right*— I knew something was wrong before."

When I changed my own game, at the age of 45, and adopted what I now call the Ballistic Swing, I won the New England Senior Tennis Championship two years in a row, surprising my best friends, my worst enemies, my wife, and myself. Over the past few years I have discussed my theories with literally hundreds of people, including some of the world's greatest players and coaches. Some of them have agreed privately, some have been just stunned, and some have attempted to disagree—but always without reasons. I hope I am a reasonable man. When someone has proven me wrong on my tennis theories, I will put them back whence they came. But in the meantime, I'll stick with the ballistic!

15.

Summary: 50 things to remember

1. Don't let the racket start forward before the ball bounces.
2. Watch the ball very carefully *after* it bounces, and adjust your swing on unexpected bounces.
3. On all shots, get your weight going forward, not sideways or backwards (except on off-the-court shots or those that force you back).
4. Step forward on the right foot for all forehands, if possible.
5. Contact the ball opposite the right hip on forehands.
6. Step forward on the left foot for all backhands, if possible.
7. Contact the ball slightly ahead of the left hip on backhands.

8. Develop a one-piece swing—body and arm in sequence.
9. On drives, hit the ball on the rise or at the top of the bouce whenever possible.
10. Remember that follow-through determines the direction of the shot.
11. Get the ball over the net—avoid "gift" points.
12. On groundstrokes, aim between service line and baseline.
13. Take a full pivot on all groundstrokes and serves.
14. Feel the ball hit the center of the racket.
15. Aim your serves and strokes above the net.
16. Rest the racket in your idle hand between all shots.
17. Grip the racket firmly only at contact.
18. Lob when your opponent is in close or when playing for position.
19. Conceal the direction of your shot until the last moment.
20. On backhands the racket strings are up at the end of the backswing.
21. Sweep the ball rather than hit it on the groundstrokes and full volleys.
22. Hit the ball firmly with confidence, and accelerate the racket on contact.
23. Balls that hit the net generally have been contacted too far forward. Change the bevel of the racket if necessary.
24. Use top-spin for control.
25. Hit flat for speed.
26. Contact the ball in the hitting zone—don't hit too far in front and don't let balls get behind you.

27. Get your racket back in time to swing it forward without hurrying.

28. On the smash, get the racket down back and right foot forward.

29. Keep the elbow low on the backswing to avoid an unnecessary loop.

30. Use a two-hand backswing on the backhand.

31. On low backhands, be sure to bend the knees for an easier pivot.

32. Bend the knees in proportion to the height of the ball.

33. Slice high backhands.

34. Keep the back of the hand *up* for the backhand.

35. Keep the top of the hand slightly *forward* for the sliced backhand.

36. On the serve, hit the ball *before* it reaches the top of the toss with an upward, outward, and forward swing.

37. On the serve, point the toes to the net before the hit.

38. Toss the ball for service with the palm of the left hand facing toward the right sideline.

39. Be sure the racket drops down the back on service.

40. Keep the right elbow high on the serve.

41. Keep the wrist loose on the serve.

42. Toss the ball above your head on the serve and hit at the beginning of the swing with backhand grip.

43. On an extreme backhand grip toss the ball to the left of the head.

44. Practice the volley from the service line.

45. Punch balls in front on volleys—motion is forward and down.

46. Keep the elbows high on volleys above the net.

47. Balls bouncing at the feet should be half-volleyed.
48. Balls in between the half volley and the longer, normal bounce must be watched very carefully and hit with precision.
49. Concentrate harder on important points, and don't get behind because of carelessness—a net-cord or wood shot can beat you.
50. Remember, the racket is a precision instrument, not a club.

Conclusion: What this system does for you

1. It establishes the correct sequence of motion, making each shot more instinctive.
2. By hitting from a standardized position, you conceal the direction of the shot.
3. My system standardizes the power used on 98% of all shots, giving greater accuracy.
4. It eliminates timing, because the feet control the exact point of contact.
6. It shortens the backswing for greater accuracy and longer follow-through for improved direction.
7. It enables the player to keep *both* eyes on the ball and to see more clearly the position of his opponent.
8. It makes controlled speed possible by establishing the correct relationship between arm and body.

9. It allows for a smoother swing from a wound-up body pivot.
10. It provides the correct foot position for the serve, directing the arm naturally to the right spot for the toss and winding up the body to the correct position for the hit.
11. It establishes a definite rhythm for the serve, causing all the elements of this usually difficult stroke to fall into proper sequence.
12. It proves that the best footwork is the least footwork, thereby conserving stamina, so necessary in a long match.
13. It is less apt to cause "tennis elbow" by providing for a smooth swing without strain.
14. It reveals the source of power on all strokes, a basic principle easily learned within five minutes.
15. By standarizing the basic strokes and making them easier, it allows the pupil to develop refinements naturally.
16. It allows the player to concentrate on strategy by making the strokes instinctive.
17. It teaches correct tennis principles, thereby making the variables of the game easier to master.
18. It allows the player to hit sharper angles on serve, backhand, forehand, and volley, because the ball is hit earlier.
19. It allows the player to be one full step closer to the net.